PASSIVE INCOME

&

KINDLE PUBLISHING:

HOW TO SUCCESSFULLY CREATE A PASSIVE

INCOME ONLINE

Daniel Shepherd

INTRODUCTION

For centuries, book publishing has been something that only those who were truly dedicated to getting their works in printed form have invested time and money into doing. It was something only the most ardent writers and academics did because the process was long, tedious, and potentially costly. With the advent of ebooks, all of that has changed.

No one has mastered the art of ebook publishing like Amazon. Using the Amazon Kindle Direct Publishing, it is possible for anyone with an idea and a bit of extra time to generate passive income from publishing books. Even better – you don't have to be a writer to do it. While it does take dedication and a willingness to manage the project, once the project is complete you can continue to make money long after the book is available on the market.

You should not plan to use your published book as a sole source of income. Rather, Kindle Direct Publishing offers a way to make additional money from home – in other words, without having to take a second job on someone else's time line. You have complete control of each project, from the subject to marketing to the timeframe.

Essentially, Amazon Kindle Direct Publishing gives you a chance to turn an idea into a book, and for you to turn that book into income. It will take planning and you will want to hire at least one or two people to help you, but ultimately it is considerably cheaper and easier than nearly any other method of extra cash. You also get the added benefit of having accomplished something when you are done.

This book will help you navigate the different elements so that you can turn your idea and free time into extra earnings.

Table of Contents

Introduction

Chapter 1. Setting Realistic

Expectation

Chapter 2. Picking a Topic and Getting Started

   Topics – Choosing from the Endless Possibilities

      The Kindle Direct Publishing Website

      Starting with Research

      Starting with Your Interests

      Finish Your Selection

   The Budget

   Setting a Timeline

Chapter 3. Tools

   Kindle Tools

   Templates

   Editing

Chapter 4. Writing

   Considerations for Doing It Yourself

   Considerations for Attributing the Work to the Writer

   Considerations for Ghost Writers

Chapter 5. Finding a GhostWriter

   Writer Platforms

     Upwork

     Guru

     All Indie Writers

     Fiverr

     Staff.com

     Other Platforms

   Negotiating Price

Chapter 6. Getting the Right Look

Book Cover

Do You Need Pictures?

Black and White Vs. Color Pictures

Maps

On Free Pictures

Should I Find a Specialist?

Chapter 7. Marketing & Pricing

Before Publication

Reviewers

Setting a PRICE for the Initial

Release

Chapter 8. Editing

Why You Have to Have an Editor

Editor Platforms

Negotiating Price

Chapter 9. Publishing on

Amazon

  Preparation

  Uploading Your Book

Chapter 10. Tips & Tricks

  Learn from Others

  Have a Loyalty Plan

  Monitor Your Metrics

  Periodically Review Publications

  Be Cautious About Revisions

CHAPTER 1. SETTING REALISTIC EXPECTATION

To start your project off right, you have to set realistic expectations. From the amount of time it will take to complete your project until you receive your expected earnings, you have to understand what passive earnings are and what kind of investment it will take to get even a modest return.

For example, if you aren't willing to put much time into it, you will need to compensate by putting more money into the publication. If you prefer to do more of the work yourself, then you can get by with a smaller budget. If you pick a topic that is not popular with a large audience, then it isn't going to matter how much time or money you put into the effort, it is not likely you will get much on the return.

This is why it is important to select a topic that is likely to sell (or that has a niche that you can market to), and to involve people who know how to work toward your intended audience. You also need to know who your audience is. If you pick a subject that is interesting to you, you already have an idea of the type of people who will be interested. However, you need to research how well received books on the topic have been in the past.

For example, if you are interested in a work of fiction, romance and horror are the most popular stories currently. That also means that quite a large number of people are trying to make money from these genres. The romance and horror genres are saturated with new publications every day. If you plan to enter this market, you need to keep your expectations low on the return of money. Then again, you will probably be able to hire a small staff at a much lower rate since there are numerous writers, editors, and marketers available, and they have to lower their costs to be competitive.

If you are more interested in publishing a book that is nonfiction, you need to decide on a subject. Self-help books are incredibly common, so that will be a difficult market if you are looking to earn longer-term passive income. There are plenty of how-to topics, theories, and even poems that you can publish.

You should know what the average income is on the topic you choose, but you also need to consider the other aspects of the project. Your budget is one of the biggest considerations because it is usually the limiting factor.

The other major aspect is typically the amount of available time. You need to know what kind of time-frame you want to follow before beginning because you will need to communicate that to everyone involved. This also means determining how many people you want to involve in the process. Naturally, all of these things affect your budget, and ultimately determine the success of your book.

All of these elements are important and you need to know them so that you can establish realistic expectations for your publication. It is easy to get caught up in your project and to over estimate how much you will earn. You need to stay focused and keep your expectations aligned with the performance of other books in the genre. This will help you to estimate your return on the publication more realistically.

CHAPTER 2. PICKING A TOPIC AND GETTING STARTED

The biggest challenge you will face is finding a topic that you can publish. As mentioned in the previous chapter, you have to know the market for your idea, as well as selecting a subject that is likely to sell. There is literally an entire world of possibilities (and if you are writing fiction, there were many worlds).

The key is to find something that you enjoy, or at least don't mind spending a lot of time working with, and one that other people are interested in reading about. This sounds like it would be easy, but if that were the case, *everyone* would be in the publishing business. The truth is, selecting a topic is going to be the most important aspect of the publication as it will ultimately guide your success.

Topics – Choosing from the Endless Possibilities

You can start with either one of two ways to select your subject:

- Research the best selling books to get ideas about topics and genres
- List your favorite subjects, hobbies, or areas of interest (include things you would like to learn about)

The first method will help you narrow your topic based on what is currently popular, while the second helps you focus on an area of interest to yourself. Most people start with the former because you want to ensure you make money after investing time and funds into the publication. However, you should not discount the benefits of the second option.

In the end, you will have to do both steps, but you will have a different set of topics to consider for the second step. When it comes to picking a topic, these are really the two most important areas because if you don't like the subject, the schedule is likely to falter or the project to fall apart. Besides, it's a side project, so you really should find some enjoyment in it. If you pick a subject that no one else is interested in reading, it's not going to matter how much time and effort you put into the project, you aren't going to make a good return on your time and money.

THE KINDLE DIRECT PUBLISHING WEBSITE
Regardless of which option you use to select your topic, the first place you should go is the Kindle Direct Publishing - https://kdp.amazon.com/ . Sign up for an account and bookmark it.

Right on the first page, Amazon covers all of the major genres and helps you start to focus on a specific topic. Reading through what is available here will help you determine where you would like to begin. You may be inspired to learn more about a subject that is covered by one of the genres, and since it is published on the site, you already know that there is an audience for your topic and it is easy to find out how big the audience is.

The site lists the following as the most popular genres on the platform (giving you a head start in researching since you already know what sells well for your target publishing medium):

- Business and investing
- Comics
- EDU
- Kids
- Fiction
- Mystery and Thriller
- Non-fiction
- Romance
- Sci-fi

- Young Adult

By clicking on the links, you are taken to a short list of authors and the success they have found through that particular genre. You will want to come back later when you are ready to get started publishing your book. Of course, you aren't quite to that stage yet, so for now you are done with the site. Save this area for later when you are ready to publish.

STARTING WITH RESEARCH

After the Amazon site, Google is your next best bet to getting a list of possible subjects for your ebook. You can run searches like "best selling books 2016" to get book titles and reviews on the books that have recently entered the market.

The reason to start with research is that you rule out areas that are less likely to sell before you invest any time or money in them. You can quickly determine the ideas that are likely to yield a better passive income.

The biggest flaw with this method is that you are looking at topics that have already recently been published, which means you are entering a market where further works on the subject may not be welcome or lucrative. So even if it is an area of interest to others, your audience may not welcome yet another book on the subject.

One way around this is to read the reviews of the current books to see why people were disappointed with them or what flaws were in the books. You could find success in addressing the deficiencies, and since your book will appear for the search results in that genre, you will gain more attention.

STARTING WITH YOUR INTERESTS

While this is meant to be passive income, you definitely do not want to force yourself to work on something you have little to no interest in, and certainly not something you cannot enjoy or tolerate. After all, you will be asked questions about it, and if you are obviously disinterested in your own work, people are going to notice.

If you start by listing the hobbies and areas of interest to yourself, you are much more likely to arrive at your desired topic faster. It is much easier to research when you already have your ideas narrowed down to a few fields. You can also then focus your search on those few areas to see how the books have performed for the past few years. For example, vampire and zombie stories are very cyclical – once a decade or so, they are quite popular. If the topics have been popular with the reading public within the last few years, it is best to avoid them as people are burnt out after the flurry of these stories.

Nonfiction doesn't sell as well as fiction, but it does sell for a lot longer (unless you write about technology, which constantly changes, making books out of date within a couple years of publication). That means that nonfiction work will give you a longer period of passive income than a work of fiction, even if it doesn't bring in as much initially.

The problem with starting with your interests is that you could miss areas that sell well that you could find interesting. By focusing solely on areas that you are currently interested in, you are ignoring large swatches of topics that may be of interest to potential readers. This does not mean that people won't be interested in your work - it simply means you could be eliminating some genres or styles you would enjoy working with that are more appealing to readers.

FINISH YOUR SELECTION

Once you've compiled a list (whether based on research or on your interests), narrow down the topic based on the second point. This is a much simpler process if you started with the research because it takes very little time to say you are or are not interested in something. It may take a little longer to research areas that you find interesting, but you will spend less time researching in the long run since you have a focused list instead of starting with a wide open field.

THE BUDGET

Once you have a topic, it's time to establish a budget. This is one of the most painful aspects as there are things you don't know for certain yet, and if you are seeking to earn passive income, you probably don't have a lot of money to put into the effort. There are several considerations that you need to take into your budget:

- Who many of the following people do you plan to hire?
    - Ghostwriter
    - Editor

- Graphic designer
- Marketer
- An experienced Amazon publisher

- What is the current average rate of compensation for people in these positions?
- What level of expertise do you want your contractors to have?
- How much of the work can you do yourself?

It is entirely possible that there can be zero cost to publishing, but that is not ideal. You can get by without hiring someone for most of the positions, but you really do need at least an editor. If that is the only position you hire, you can put all of the budget into finding an editor that you can work well with and make it a long-term relationship for later books. If you need to hire a writer, the majority of your budget is going to go to that writer, no matter how many other people you hire. Ghostwriters give up all rights to the books they create, and the ones who can write something that will sell are going to charge you before they turn over the rights.

Besides an editor, you really want to consider getting marketing help. Amazon can help you there, so look into the different options to determine your marketing budget.

If the only image you need is the cover, there are plenty of free images (including some provided by Amazon), so you won't need a graphic designer. If you are working on a comic/manga or children's book and want to add pictures, or if you are working on fantasy and want to include a map, you will need to add a considerable chunk of the budget for your graphic artist. There may be a lot of them, but the ones worth hiring want to be paid a reasonable amount for their services (like the writer, they are turning over their

work to you without receiving credit for their work–
that will cost a bit).

Amazon Direct Publishing is simple enough that you
really shouldn't need help. There are many different
platforms where you can get assistance, including on
the site itself (which is always the best starting point).
However, if you are pressed for time, you can build
help into your budget. It should not be too costly since
it is simple, but you will want to do some research to
see what the going rate for assistance is before com-
mitting part of your budget for publishing assistance.

SETTING A TIMELINE

While it may seem nonsensical, you need to establish
a timeline before you hire anyone. Essentially, you are
the boss, so whatever time frame you want to meet
will be the goal of all those you employ to assist you.

Every Kindle Direct Publishing project is unique, but here are a few guidelines for you to consider when establishing your schedule.

1. Your timeframe needs to be realistic. If this is your first publication, you are going to need to add extra time as a buffer to make sure you have time to properly manage the different aspects of publication. Everything is going to take longer than you think it will, so pad your schedule from the beginning.

2. The timeline needs to cover each phase of the project following selecting the idea and establishing a budget.

3. Editing will need at least half the amount of time as the writing. Too often people shortchange the editing process, and that can have disastrous results (like releasing a video game with a lot of bugs in it). Readers are willing to

overlook a few errors, but if your book is full of typos and grammatical errors, this is going to be one of the first call outs in the review and will discourage others from purchasing your book. Your editor will need longer than you think to properly go through the book. A good editor will go through your work two or three times before returning it. While it doesn't take as long to read and edit as it does to write, it does take a considerable amount of time to do it right.

4. You can work on several things at the same time. For example, if you hire a ghostwriter, as the book is being written, you can be selecting the cover and any corresponding images. If you are the writer, you can do all of this while the editor is going through the work. As mentioned in the previous point, you will have plenty of

time, and since you wrote the book, you are going to find that selecting the images is considerably easier than if it is written by someone else.

5. If you write the book yourself, you need to at least double the amount of time to write. Though many people learn to write at a young age, there are only a few people to whom writing comes naturally. This does not mean you are a bad writer, it just means that it is likely to take you considerably longer to finish your first book or two than someone who writes all of the time. And this is not a bad thing – it is just a major consideration you need to think about when creating your timeline.

Chapter 3. Tools

In addition to being able to publish books on their own (for free), writers and those looking for passive income have a wide range of tools readily available to help get their book completed and ready for public consumption. From the appearance and formatting to editing and marketing, there are a wealth of tools that can ensure that your book is in the best shape possible when you publish it.

Naturally, Kindle has a healthy tool kit that gives you most of the assistance you need. If you want to make your book stand out or appear different to the other Kindle books, there are other tools available for self-publishers.

Kindle Tools

First things first, you need to create an account with Kindle Direct Publishing - https://kdp.amazon.com/ .

Go through all of their promotional information and basic information about the benefits of publishing with Kindle. It will help you better understand the process before you get into the details.

The best place to start is on the Kindle Direct Publishing Help page - https://kdp.amazon.com/help?ref_=kdp_AC_TN_help . This page shows you the types of tools available, and some of them go well beyond just getting the book published (like royalty monitoring and reporting tools – yes, you will be able to pull statements from this site come tax season, making it much easier to get your taxes done).

There are two areas of interest on this page for getting your book published:

- Publish, which includes help topics on everything related to getting your book published

- Promote, which helps you get the word out there about your book

Take the time to go through these topics for a lot of information that will be useful later on.

Run a search for Tools.

The results will include all of the different divisions (genres) that are possible for publication, including Japanese illustrated books (under Kindle Kid's Book Creator), textbooks (Kindle Textbook Creator), and formatting assistance (KindleGen v2.9). The types of tools you need depends on the kind of book you want to publish (already your topic is affecting how much work you have and what you need to do).

What this means is that every time you want to write a book on a different genre, you will need to come back and read over all of the information specific to the genre you are working in.

Tools are also divided up by your platform.

- PC users can go here - https://kdp.amazon.com/help?topicId=A1B6GKJ79HC7AN for tips and tricks about formatting and dealing with every-thing needed to prepare a book for publication. They are very thorough, so set aside half a day to really go over what they have listed.

- Mac users can go here - https://kdp.amazon.com/help?topicId=A2AOXJXY43GME3 for information on creating and previewing ebooks, as well as getting some advanced techniques. You will also want to check out the information on the PC page since many of the tips and tricks apply to both types of platforms, you just have a bit more power to do additional stuff on a Mac – Kindle has taken that into account and created a page for you.

As far as the publication tools go, stick with Kindle because their tips and information will ensure your book has the most compatible look and feel for their platform.

Before going any further, take the time to read the [Kindle Publishing Guidelines](http://s3.amazonaws.com/kindlegen/AmazonKindlePublishingGuidelines.pdf) - http://s3.amazonaws.com/kindlegen/AmazonKindlePublishingGuidelines.pdf (if you didn't do this when you set up your account).

TEMPLATES

You should always start with a template. When you become proficient at publishing books you will actually be much more likely to use templates, especially once you've written several books. Templates have many different advantages, but most importantly they ensure your formatting is consistent throughout and that your book is divided into sections that are easy to follow. You may not want to run your life on a template, but when it comes to working with the same kind of file, a template is essential. There are actually a lot (and I mean A LOT) of free templates out there.

Run a Google search for Kindle publishing templates and you will have many, many pages worth of free templates you can use. Pick the one that you like and meets your needs the best; however, here are a few things to keep in mind as you go through the templates:

- Keep it as simple as possible.

- Most of these templates really aren't designed for picture books – stick to the help Kindle provides if you are adding a lot of images.

- The type of file you use should be something you can easily manage. As wonderful as Adobe products are, you don't need anything that elegant for Kindle publishing; Kindle Direct Publishing takes care of most of the formatting aspects as you add the books. The easier the file type, the quicker the formatting.

- You are welcome to modify templates to meet your specific needs. There is nothing saying you have to use them exactly as they are posted. As you publish more books, update your template or templates to meet your needs.

- Verify that the template has all of the elements you need, and this means more than just chapters and a title page. Take a few minutes to scroll through this book in its entirety – it has a number of sections you probably did not think about, like the legal section, as well a place for you to add a bio and market your other books.

If you try to write a book without a template, you will learn after writing a few books that creating a template and updating it over time is a far more efficient way to simplify the process.

EDITING

You really need to pay for someone to read over your book, whether as an editor or as a critic. No tool is going to be able to help you when it comes to the book's content.

That being said, there are a number of available tools that can help you with the purely grammatical aspects. These four sites offer a good bit of grammar support for free.

- After the Deadline - www.polishmywriting.com/ is a basic editor that checks your spelling, grammar, and can make some basic style suggestions. For your first few books, it is best to focus on the spelling and grammar and have a real person offer suggestions about style.

- Grammarly - https://app.grammarly.com provides basic grammar and spelling suggestions. You will get emails letting you know how you are doing statistically compared to their other users, too. While not required, it can remind you to switch things up and try to expand your vocabulary.

- EditMinion - http://editminion.com/ has a nifty name and it offers some inspiration (in addition to being a very handy basic editor).

- Hemingway App - http://www.hemingwayapp.com/ goes a bit further than the other editors. It will not only point out your basic errors, it will let you know your readability (what grade level you are writing to –very handy if your intended audience is younger). It's a bit more sophisticated, looks a bit more professional, but can be overwhelming if you are not a fan of color coding and feeling like you are being judged.

Chapter 4. Writing

The next big question is about the writing. Do you plan to write the book yourself or pay someone else to do it? If you plan to pay someone else to write the book, will you give the writer credit, or do you want to have all of the rights to the work yourself? If you do not want to give the writer credit, that means you are looking for a ghostwriter.

This chapter looks at the pros and cons of each of these options to help you determine how you want to manage the biggest chunk of work.

Considerations for Doing It Yourself

You really don't need to know the pros and cons of writing it yourself – just ask yourself one question – "Am I a good writer?" If you answered no to that question, don't even consider writing the book yourself.

Skip to the next two sections to determine if you want to use a ghostwriter or not.

If you are at least a decent writer, you will need to decide if you want to write the book yourself.

- Are you already an expert in the subject? If so, it is usually best to do it yourself. You know best what points you want to make and dealing with another writer could be very frustrating – not because of the writer but because you already know what you want to say. It may take a long time to try to explain to a writer what you want, then there is the review process, and other items. If you know the subject well, at least develop the chapters and outline what you want. If it takes too long, then look for a writer. Your ideas will already be down, taking most of the guesswork out of the process.

- Do you have time to complete the project within your schedule? If not, or if you find your schedule keeps slipping because of other projects in your life taking priority, find someone to do the writing for you. Writing your book will be a priority for the writer because it is their job, whereas it is more of a side project for you.

- What do you hope to get out of the book? If it is a topic that you want to learn more about, you benefit either way. Doing the writing yourself means you will be doing a lot of research, but you will not have an expert to scrutinize what you say. If you hire a writer, you will lose out on learning from research, but you will be able to test and try what they write – there's nothing like an expert's perspective to give a project focus.

- If you are working on a book of fiction, do you already have an idea for the story? Do you already have characters and events mapped out, or more a vague notion? If you don't know details, a writer can pick up on basic ideas and create whole worlds you may not have even considered – it's what they do for a living, giving them a distinct advantage over people who do it recreationally. However, nothing makes up for your own inspiration. Some of the most famous writers wrote as a hobby, so decide what you hope to get out of the work and how close you are to your characters and the events. This will tell you whether you should hire someone to help or take on the writing yourself as a labor of love.

CONSIDERATIONS FOR ATTRIBUTING THE WORK TO THE WRITER

The primary benefit of giving credit to a writer for the work is that you may end up paying far less for the services. If you pay a flat rate for the project, writers who do not have a large portfolio are much more likely to be agreeable to a small budget just to get their name out there. More experienced writers will probably negotiate on the royalties, which won't cost you very much if the book doesn't sell well. If the book does do well though, you may be looking at splitting a considerable sum with the writer. Then again, it is passive income and your part was in managing the project – odds are high that the writer did far more work than you in the end, which is why experienced writers are more willing to gamble on their work.

CONSIDERATIONS FOR GHOST WRITERS

Ghostwriting is one of the most common ways of getting books written. There is a huge pool of writers willing to hand over the rights to their work because (for the most part) the writing isn't an area they are interested in. There aren't many jobs for writers that give them credit for their work and where the pay that they do get is good, so it's an easy way for a good writer to get extra income. There are many reasons people will ghostwrite instead of publishing themselves (letting you gamble on the book's success is one reason – they get paid either way), but their reasons really don't matter in terms of your project.

What does matter is finding a ghostwriter who can turn your idea into a book that is likely to sell. If you want to publish a book on learning a programming language but don't know any programming, you can find someone who does know programming and is willing to write the book for you for a fee. If you have an idea for a story but don't know how to develop it, this is one of the most saturated markets to find a good ghostwriter to do the work (almost all writers want to get paid to write fiction). A writer will negotiate a rate, and then get started turning your idea into book.

There are two things you should keep in mind about ghostwriters.

- They have no vested interest in the success of your book once it is done. If you want revisions or changes after publication, you will probably have to pay the writer again to get it done – and if the book was successful, the writer is going to charge you a LOT more to make the changes.

- They are very driven by your deadlines because that determines their pay. They are more likely to make sure you can pay before beginning, and will ask a lot more questions, forcing you to really think about the book, which is a great way to make you think ahead. Their questions may seem a bit annoying at first, but they want to get it right the first time so that they don't waste their time and yours. As long as they meet the expectations set at the beginning, they will expect you to pay at the end, and you are not likely to get additional work without further costs.

While they have the least investment in your book, ghostwriters tend to be extremely reliable because the book is a job, not the potential for additional income.

Chapter 5. Finding a GhostWriter

If you decide you want to hire a ghostwriter, this will likely be the most difficult aspect of the project. You have to find someone that you work well with, as well as someone who is a good writer.

Fortunately, there are a lot of platforms out there listing writers who are willing and able to ghostwriter for you.

Writer Platforms

There are a large number of available platforms where you can find a writer because there are a lot of writers out there. And like writers, not all of the platforms are equal or able to provide you with what you need.

A quick word about finding a writer in a globalized market – cheaper doesn't always mean better, it just means cheaper. This means you can find a writer in your country (or who understands the culture and unique spelling/idioms), but it also means you are going to get quite a few people who claim to be able to write but don't speak English as their first language. The problem with that is that they are willing to write for far less than someone who can really do your book justice, and that is so appealing when you focus on the budget. Don't fall for it. You will end up spending more when you have to hire a native English speaker to clean it up, or more likely entirely re-do it. Fortunately, you can set the criteria and automatically eliminate those who are less familiar with the language. You also need to keep in mind that the average cost for a native speaker is considerably higher, so you will need to be realistic about the cost. If you don't offer a decent wage for the work, you are not going to get the kind of writer who can help you turn the book into passive income.

Here are five of the most popular platforms for businesses and writers. Take some time to get familiar with them before you sign up and hire a writer. Also, pay attention to the rates so that you can make a realistic budget for the project. If you under-budget the posting, you are not going to get the caliber writer you want.

UPWORK

Upwork - https://www.upwork.com is perhaps the biggest name in the freelancing world and it is an international platform.

The site does have a huge pool of potential writers, both ghostwriting and non-ghostwriting. You will need a decent description and a deadline, but the platform will manage communications, payment, and deadlines for you. Writers enjoy the site because it ensures they are paid on time (and that you have the agreed upon rate to pay them for their work).

You can use this site to find more than just a writer too. If you want to hire an editor, marketer, or someone to manage the publication portion, you can post jobs for those positions too, and manage all of your freelance workers from one place.

GURU

Guru - http://www.guru.com/ is like Upwork because it has a wealth of other freelancing services, such as websites and coding. You can review potential writers, invite them to bid on your project, and manage payment and deadlines over the platform. All of the tools you need are on the site so that you don't have to worry about working through multiple apps or programs to get the job done.

ALL INDIE WRITERS

All Indie Writers - http://allindiewriters.com/ is the only site listed here that is exclusively for writers, but it isn't the only one out there (you can also check out is WriterAccess - http://www.writeraccess.com/ , which is exclusively American freelance writers). One of the benefits of using this site is that you cut out having to wade through a lot of unrelated information. The writers on the site are pretty serious, and you are much less likely to find a writer who does not speak English natively. You can post your job for a small fee, or you can choose a writer from the directory. It's a nice set up that is geared specifically to writing.

FIVERR

Fiverr - https://www.fiverr.com/ is unique in that you review all of the potential candidates based on what they are willing to do for $5. Read through their postings, see what is included for the $5 rate (such as $5 for 100 words or $5 to post a positive review about the book). While you are not going to find a writer for a complete ebook for $5, you can get an idea of how much they charge per word. You can also find people to market your work or provide an interesting book cover for relatively cheap here. It may take a bit longer to go through everything, but if you are specific in your criteria, it can really pay off because you are chhttps://www.staff.com/oosing the writer instead of passively reviewing bids.

STAFF.COM

Staff.com - https://www.staff.com/ is similar to Upwork, meaning you have decent controls over the presentation of your project and the tools to manage it. You can also hire people to fill other positions. Typically, the site works with companies, and not one time projects, but if you plan on publishing ebooks on a regular basis, it might be worth the time to check them out.

You can also try some of the more common job platforms, like Indeed and Craigslist. Just be aware that since these boards are not catering just to freelancers or writing, you are taking a much greater gamble on finding the writer you need.

NEGOTIATING PRICE

There are two ways to pay ghostwriters – fixed rate or by the hour. If you are sticking to a tight budget, fixed rate is the best option. If you are looking for a long-term project that will take a few months to complete, it may be best to work by the hour. You may need to establish guidelines for the timeframe and you will definitely need open communication for an hourly rate.

In the beginning, stick with the fixed rate. You can get many good writers for a fixed rate, and that will help you learn the ropes, the amount of time it takes to complete the work, and gives you one fewer concern while you are trying to find your groove.

CHAPTER 6. GETTING THE RIGHT LOOK

No doubt you have heard the saying about not judging a book by the cover for most of your life, but people still do. The way you present the book will play a huge role in the number of people who will be interested in it. You also need to plan for the way you present the book and make sure that it is consistently formatted (see Chapter 3 about templates).

BOOK COVER

Just because you are writing an ebook doesn't mean you can ignore the cover or be cavalier about it. Book covers tell your potential readers a lot about the book. If you have a picture of a man and a woman on the cover, people will expect the book to be a romance story and probably won't even read the description if that isn't what they are interested in. If you have dragons, magical symbols, or swords, readers will assume the book is about fantasy. What you put on the cover really does help determine how many members of the public buy it in the early days following publication.

Pick something that hints at what is in the book but that intrigues potential readers to go through the description. Your book cover is the first selling point – use that to your advantage.

DO YOU NEED PICTURES?

This may not be as straightforward an answer as you may think. There are plenty of famous books that have pictures within the pages, so you shouldn't think that you don't need pictures just because you are doing a work of nonfiction or a serious story.

Most nonfiction books actually require several pictures. Readers need those pictures to illustrate how to do something, as a point of reference or clarification, or just out of curiosity. If your topic is nonfiction, the question isn't whether you need pictures, it's about where will pictures be most beneficial.

If you are working on a story, it is much less likely that you will need pictures. However, readers love maps and character charts, which are pictures. If your story is long with a number of characters or if a map of the area/world/building will be helpful, plan to add it. Fandoms often take these items and run with them.

BLACK AND WHITE VS. COLOR PICTURES MAPS

Regardless of the type of book, if you plan to add maps, you need to consider whether they should be black and white or colored. Black and white is cheaper, even though it isn't printed, but it is not always the best option. Ultimately, it depends on what your map is meant to show. If you have a legend and a lot of detail, make it easier for your reader and go with color.

ON FREE PICTURES

If pictures are an important part of your book (like kid's books or comics), this is not an option for you. You must have an artist (or be the artist).

Hiring an artist to illustrate your book is every bit as difficult as hiring a writer, and just as expensive. If you have the budget for it, it is best to get an artist. Artists can take your idea and turn it into something amazing, all based on your words.

If you have a really tight budget and only need a couple of pictures, finding them for free is a possible option. To find free art, you need to look up images that are licensed for free use as long as the artist is attributed. If you find an image you love but aren't sure if you can use it, contact the artist.

If no artist is listed, don't use the picture.

That said, there are a few sites that have images that you can use for free as long as you attribute the image to the artist or photographer (they will always be listed for every image):

- Stock.xchang - http://www.freeimages.com/
- Flickr - www.flickr.com (you will need to browse only the images listed under the advanced search criteria of Creative Commons)
- Wikimedia Commons - https://commons.wikimedia.org/wiki/Main_Page (the source for most Wikipedia pictures)

Before using any photos or art from these sites, make sure you read the rules of use. If you have any doubt, contact the artist. It would actually be very nice if you notify the artist even if it is fine to use the image just so the person knows how the work is being used. Who knows, the artist may tell friends about your book.

SHOULD I FIND A SPECIALIST?

If you are wondering if you need someone who specializes in book covers or images, chances are the answer is yes. Kindle does have a lot of interesting options for book covers, so you can start there, but anything beyond that and you may want someone who knows a good deal about catching people's attention through art.

If you need a map for your book, you definitely need a specialist (that specialist may be someone you already know who has expressed an interest in doing this sort of thing). If you need other images inside the book, start with the free resources.

Don't forget, you can always take your own pictures. That is always free and you know that your ebook can use the image.

If you need charts and character trees, you may be able to do this yourself too. They will need to look nice, but they don't need to be complicated, and it is best to err on the side of over simplistic so that the images are functional. People want to use them for their information over having something that looks good but that they can't read.

Chapter 7. Marketing & Pricing

Marketing is the one aspect that most people don't want to think about doing because it requires a lot of time and effort. However, it isn't something you have to do alone.

Before Publication

Marketing begins after the writing is well under way and you have a book cover. You want to make sure you have an idea of when the book will be ready for the public before you really begin marketing it.

It is equally important to do a lot of marketing before the ebook is published. This can mean working on making it available through preorder, but really it is a lot more than that. You need to dedicate time to really getting the word out about your book since you want this to be a nice source of passive income.

You need to create a presence for your book on social media, particularly Facebook and Twitter. People can begin to follow you and the work and start generating talk about it. As you publish more books, your followers here will help grow your audience. You can pay people to do reviews and to help you market your book (Fiverr is a great source for finding people who will help market your work fairly inexpensively), but nothing beats a steady fandom who freely promote your ebooks. It also proves that not all of your fans are paid to give you positive reviews.

If you have time, go ahead and create a website for your eBooks, especially if you are doing a series. This is particularly important for making sure that you get the kind of website people are most likely to visit to read up on your works. Whether you use your name, the name of your series, or a company name, you want to have the right domain.

You will need to keep a schedule for posting updates, regardless of the medium. Social media sites will need to be updated two or three times a week. The website should be updated at least once a quarter, but usually it is best to post something once a week, such as a blog so that it is always looks current.

If you add a discussion board for talking about your work, make sure you have control over the area and set rules for the kind of discussions and language that is allowed. Make this information visible to anyone who uses the page. Trolls are a problem, even for marketing purposes, so be prepared to kick people off of the page (and make sure you have built this functionality into the website before you go live).

REVIEWERS

Reviews play almost as big a role as the description. If a potential reader likes the description, that person is probably doing to go further and read what other people have had to say about the ebook before purchasing it.

You can pay people to read the book and post information to Amazon about it. For the best results, tell reviewers to be honest, but this also means you may have some reviews that you don't like. This is one reason having a couple of people read the book to critique it before release is important. They can point out the issues, inconsistencies, and ways to improve it before the book goes to the general public.

If you have created a social media presence and website, make sure these sites have reviews too. Get people excited about the current publication and point them to where they can purchase it from Amazon. Your best bet for continued exposure is from the reviews on these sites and Amazon. Essentially, these are your primary marketing strategy after the initial release.

SETTING A PRICE FOR THE INITIAL RELEASE

Setting a price for the book is one of the trickiest aspects, and it's something you need to properly research and consider well ahead of publication. Kindle actually has the best advice for setting the price of your Kindle Publishing Direct ebook (after all, they have the statistics on what works and what doesn't).

- Free promotions - https://kdp.amazon.com/help?topicId=A34IQ0W14ZKXM9

- Countdown deals - https://kdp.amazon.com/help?topicId=A3288N75MH14B8

- Merchandising tips - https://kdp.amazon.com/help?topicId=A37SMD4NYVZDI7

- Setting the right price - https://kdp.amazon.com/help?topicId=A3KL1PS548IZK2

Take the time to go over all of these pages to get a full understanding of the cost and what is likely to work. Keep in mind, the more experience you have, the more room you have for charging higher rates – but in the beginning, you need to set a price that will make the book more appealing. If a potential reader sees that you are a new author, but your ebook is only 99-cents, it will seem worth it to give your work a chance without losing much money on the deal. If the reader likes the book, that person is much more likely to leave a positive review and pay attention for the next one you publish.

Chapter 8. Editing

This subject has come up several times, but has not really been covered in detail. You may be wondering why an entire chapter is dedicated to something that seems so insignificant.

It's because editing **is not insignificant**.

Why You Have to Have an Editor

The kind of people who will still spend money to read a book are the kind of people who are going to pay attention to details – and not just your grammar.

If you disappoint your readers with poor grammar, an inconsistent plot, and poorly executed ideas, you will not be making a passive income off of your project.

Editors are your best defense and your best ally.

A good editor will make your book almost entirely free of grammatical errors.

A great editor will fix the grammatical errors and will point out issues with the story, as well as verify facts. An amazing editor is going to do all of this and question your ideas throughout the entire book. This kind of editor is going to give you the kind of feedback that you will get from paying customers, potentially saving you from the most basic criticisms.

Even if you have a ghostwriter, you need to pay for an editor. Writing and editing are two entirely different mindsets, and asking someone to edit their own writing is like asking a software developer to do quality assessment on their own code or asking an accountant to verify their own books. It doesn't work.

And yes, there are plenty of editing tools free and readily available online, but they don't offer what a really good editor offers. The editing tools don't give you the kind of reaction you are going to get from your flesh and blood readers.

An editor who knows how to edit will.

The Writer's Dig - http://www.writersdigest.com/on-line-editor/10-things-your-freelance-editor-might-not-tell-you-but-should has a very concise article that should prepare you for the editing process. Take the time to read it and remember what it has to say once your book is in the final stages before publication.

EDITOR PLATFORMS

You can use all of the same platforms to find an editor that you used to find a writer (or if you wrote it yourself, look through Chapter 5 to see a few of the most popular platforms with freelance writers and editors). Most importantly, find an editor who knows how to provide constructive criticism. If you hire an editor who focuses on the grammar, that is valuable, but does not give you the initial reader reaction. If you hire an editor who is abrasive, you will end up ignoring their valid suggestions because you don't like the person.

This means read the reviews others have posted on these sites about the editor. You will get an idea on how detailed an editor is just by looking over the kinds of feedback given. The best editors will have comments about being professional and thorough in their editing and feedback on the works, regardless of what the editing was for (such as website, blog, or document).

Don't forget, just because an editor hasn't done a full edit on a book does not mean the editor is not qualified. Editors tend to apply the same rules and thinking to anything they are reviewing, so regardless of their medium history, you will have a good idea of what kind of editor they are based on their reviews.

NEGOTIATING PRICE

The thing to keep in mind about editors is that they are almost always paid by the hour and their prices are seldom negotiable. This is drastically different than paying a writer, but that's because the nature of editing is significantly different than writing.

If you negotiate a price with an editor, make sure you understand what that rate means. Many editors will offer an hourly pay scale based on the kind of editing you are willing to pay them to do. For example, an editor might charge $10 an hour for a basic edit (grammar only) and up to $20 an hour for a thorough edit (including comment and consistency checks).

For nonfiction, it could be more if you hire a technical editor, but the additional cost is almost always worth it. Not only do these editors know their stuff, they will verify pretty much every fact you have in the ebook. While they can be pricey, it is worth it when your ebook becomes a reliable reference for the subject. The more accurate and complete the information you present, the more readers you will have.

Finally, editing is usually done based on the word count (it used to be page count, but that is no longer a reliable way of estimating the amount of time). For example, if you have a fictional ebook of 5,000 words, the editor will be able to estimate how long it will take to complete the edit. Editing is much easier to esti- mate than writing by word count, and that's why edi- tors tend to charge by the hour. You know roughly how long it takes to read a certain number of words (but mindset and mood seriously affect how well something is written – that's why writing based on an estimate is difficult). The more detailed you want the edit to be, the longer it will take because the editor will have to read slower, reference sources, and compare what you said in different locations within the story.

Basically, you don't get to negotiate the editor's rate – those seldom change. What you can negotiate is how detailed the edit will be. You can also start with a short project to see how well you and the editor will work together. You may or may not use the same writer for your projects, but in the end you do want to have a single editor who knows you and what you want. Over time it will result in a shorter editing process and more rewarding experience with each project.

Chapter 9. Publishing on Amazon

After all of that hard work is finally completed, it's time to get the ebook published. Compared with everything else you have had to do, this is easily the quickest part of the process, but it isn't time to celebrate just yet. You need to really focus on the process to ensure you don't miss anything or make any mistakes that are easy to avoid.

Go to the Amazon publishing guidelines - https://kdp.amazon.com/help?topicId=A2NBSNHQIHR4W3 and read through it several times before you start uploading your ebook.

You will be tempted to rush.

You will be tempted to skip steps.

You will want to get it over and get the book out there.

Don't.

This step is just as critical as everything else you have done up to this point – with the notable drawback of this step having the potential to undo most of your hard work because you were too eager or pressed to just get the project done.

If you feel like this, postpone the publication until you are more relaxed or ready to dedicate the necessary time to ensure it is done right.

PREPARATION

Once you've read through the page several times, you are ready for the final clean up.

You need to go through the formatting and make sure it meets Amazon's requirements. Then you need to make sure that it looks good on your computer (printing it to make sure everything looks good is completely unnecessary as these books are only available online – it's a different matter if you decide you also want some hardcopies of the book). All of the necessary steps to format your ebook will depend on what kind of book it is. The Amazon Simplified Formatting Guide - https://kdp.amazon.com/help?topicId=A17W8UM0MMSQX6 covers what you need for most kinds of ebooks. If you are publishing a work that has a lot of pictures, you will need to review the additional details and assistance offered for illustrated books.

Uploading Your Book

Take a minute to read and understand the Copyright Guidelines - https://kdp.amazon.com/help?topicId=A12I95WPPFYFX9 before you proceed. Make sure you understand them and that your work complies with these guidelines.

This is probably the easiest part. After you've reviewed the formatting a few times, go to your main Amazon page. It will contain a short checklist to ensure you complete all of the necessary tasks to publish your ebook, including the following:

- Uploading the ebook (as long as it is properly formatted, you will not need to do anything apart from uploading it – Amazon will convert it to the proper Kindle formatting)
- Add the book cover
- Add a description
- Determine and enter the keywords and book categories

You can use the links beside each step to ensure you get all of the details in the way you would like them to display or if you have any questions.

Once you have successfully added this information, the book will appear in the Your Books section. You can review it to make sure everything appears in the way that you intended. If anything looks wrong, click on the button *beside* the **Continue setup** button to edit or make updates.

When you are happy with the appearance, click the **Continue setup** button. You will need to add rights and territories - https://kdp.amazon.com/help?topicId=A3BZH3BNSKZoUX (make sure to read up on these because it makes your book available in countries where you have the right to publish), then set your price.

Preview all of the details one more time to make sure it looks exactly the way you want it to appear in the Kindle Store.

When everything is done, you can click on the **Save and Publish** button.

Now you are a published author.

Amazon will kindly track all of the details and will post reports so you know how much passive income you are generating from each book.

Chapter 10. Tips & Tricks

Before you publish your first book, take the time to check out what others have said. You can do this both on the Kindle Direct Publishing pages and online.

Learn from Others

The best tip is to learn from the mistakes of others. Find out what people have done that hurt sales or that they wish they had have done differently. You can easily avoid these mistakes by simply being aware of the common mistakes.

Have a Loyalty Plan

Consider ways to reward people who become loyal fans. If fans show a lot of love for a particular character, concept, or idea you've published, give them what they want – write a short story, book, or information about that character, concept or idea and then offer it for free. Hold open discussions with them in which you answer their questions. Fans love it when you acknowledge them, and even if this is a side gig or a hobby, keeping your fans happy is the best and most reliable way to improve your passive income. It usually doesn't take much, just the acknowledgement of what they have done for you. You may even get ideas about future projects from these interactions as a further bonus.

Monitor Your Metrics

Amazon makes this incredibly easy to do. Just go to your Reports page and choose one of their many options to see how each book is performing.

Periodically Review Publications

It's easy to say that once an ebook is done, you never need to think about it again, but that isn't always true. Books by Washington Irving are still being updated today, despite the fact that he died in 1859. There is always more that can be done, ideas you can add to the introduction or clarification you can add in footnotes. Kindle makes it very easy for you to post revisions too.

BE CAUTIOUS ABOUT REVISIONS

While revisions should be something you consider from time to time, they are not something you should be in the habit of doing regularly. You should not be re-publishing an ebook that was just published three days ago. That indicates that you did not properly plan or execute the final stage of the book's release, and those who bought the book are not going to be happy about a newer version being released so soon after the initial release.

Remember, revisions are not a way to clean up glaring mistakes, it's a way to perfect something that you've had many months or years to consider.

Thank you for buying and reading this book. I hope you found it useful and would love if you left comments for future improvements to the book and details about what you found most useful.

Also join up to my email list to receive special discounts and free promotions!

psiveincome@gmail.com

www.ingramcontent.com/pod-product-compliance
Lightning Source LLC
Chambersburg PA
CBHW060409190526
45169CB00002B/824